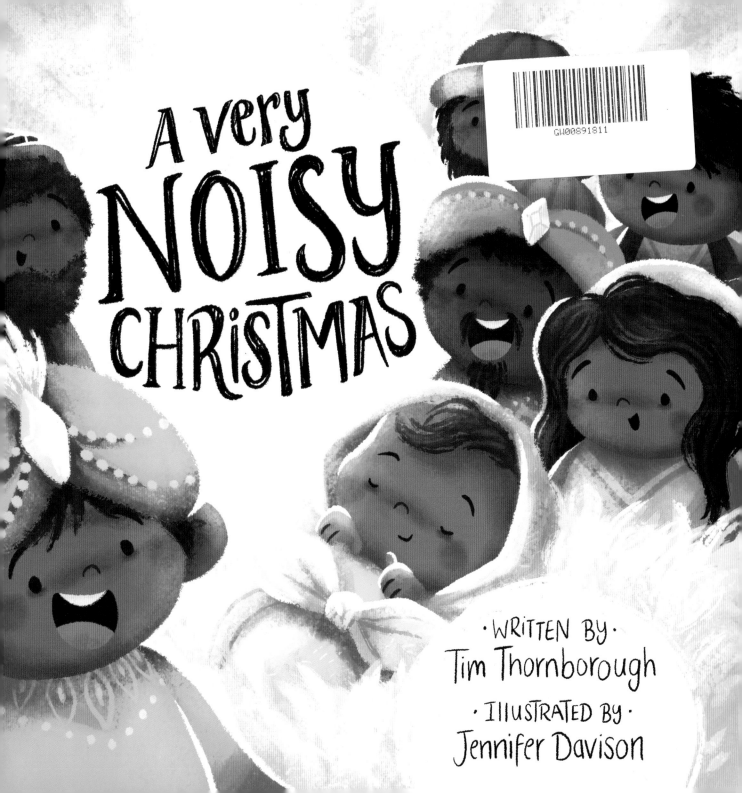

A very NOISY CHRISTMAS

·WRITTEN BY·
Tim Thornborough

·ILLUSTRATED BY·
Jennifer Davison

A Very Noisy Christmas © The Good Book Company, 2018

Words by Tim Thornborough. Illustrations by Jennifer Davison. Design and art direction by André Parker

Health Warning: this book could seriously damage your ears ... use responsibly.

UK: www.thegoodbook.co.uk North America: www.thegoodbook.com
Australia: www.thegoodbook.com.au NZ: www.thegoodbook.co.nz

ISBN: 9781784982904. Printed in Turkey

This book is a bit different from other books.

When you see words **Like THIS**
you need to say them really, REALLY loudly.

And when you see **Shhhhhhh.......**

you should whisper the words really, really quietly.

Let's practise!

Something AMAZING has happened!

Shhhhhhh.......

And if you're lucky enough to have a grown-up read
to you, make sure that they use their loudest, softest
and silliest voices!

Shhhhhhh..........

It was a quiet, quiet night on the hillside.

The shepherds and the sheep were sleeping.

Then suddenly...

AHH!
AHHHHH!
an ANGEL!

The shepherds were so, so scared.

But wait! The angel was
saying something...

Shhhhhhh.........

Let's listen carefully. The angel said,

"Don't be afraid. I bring you good news that will bring great joy to all people.

"God's Rescuer has been born in Bethlehem.

"He is the King of the whole wide wonderful world.

"You will find the baby wrapped snugly, lying in a manger."

Then suddenly...

PEACE -on- EARTH

Thousands and thousands and thousands and thousands and thousands of angels were praising God at the top of their voices!

Then suddenly...

Shhhhhhh......

The angels went back to heaven and everything was quiet again.

The shepherds hurried off to Bethlehem...

... and they found Jesus in a manger,
just like the angel had told them.

The shepherds wanted to tell everyone...

JESUS -the- RESCUER has been BORN!

Meanwhile, in a land far, far away....

... some wise men were studying
special books and watching the stars.

Then suddenly...

a new STAR had appeared in the sky!

They knew the star meant that a special King had been born.

So they packed their bags and went on a long, long, long, LOOOOOOOOONG trip to see the new King.

Shhhhhhh......

When they arrived, they found Jesus and gave him special gifts.

gold

frankincense

myrrh

They bowed down before him.

They knew he was the King of the whole wide wonderful world.

Do you want to know something special?

JESUS is God's Son -and our- RESCUER

He is the King of the whole wide wonderful world.

Jesus came at the first Christmas so we can be friends with God for ever.

Now that's something worth singing and shouting about...

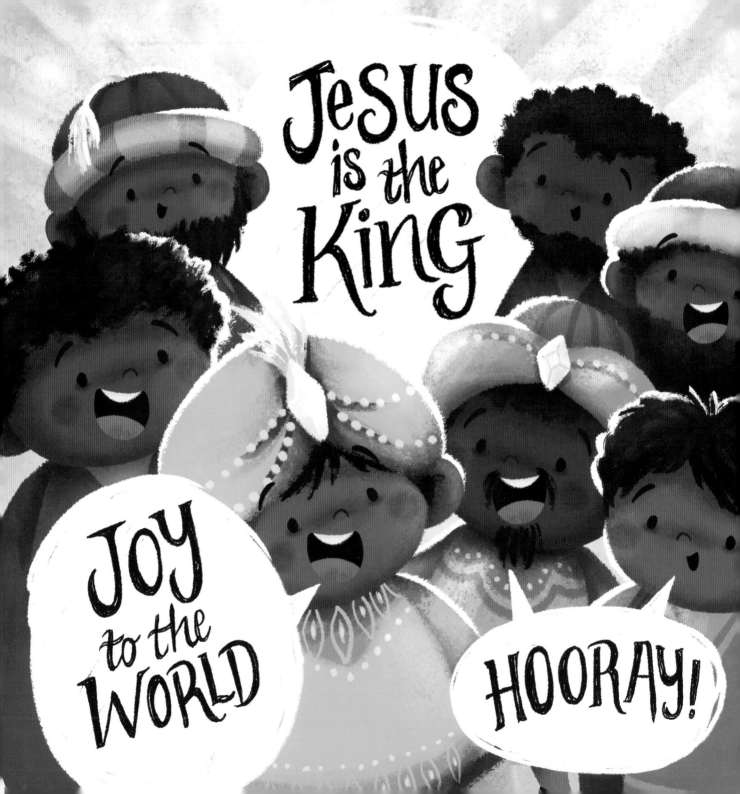